ORNAMENTATION IN
THE WORKS OF
FREDERICK CHOPIN

Da Capo Press Music Reprint Series

GENERAL EDITOR

FREDERICK FREEDMAN

VASSAR COLLEGE

ORNAMENTATION IN THE WORKS OF FREDERICK CHOPIN

By John Petrie Dunn

𝄉 DA CAPO PRESS • NEW YORK • 1971

A Da Capo Press Reprint Edition

This Da Capo Press edition of
Ornamentation in the Works of Frederick Chopin
is an unabridged republication of the first
edition published in London and New York in 1921.

Library of Congress Catalog Card Number 78-125069

SBN 306-70006-9

Published by Da Capo Press
A Division of Plenum Publishing Corporation
227 West 17th Street, New York, N.Y. 10011

ORNAMENTATION IN THE WORKS OF FREDERICK CHOPIN

NOVELLO'S
MUSIC PRIMERS AND EDUCATIONAL SERIES.

ORNAMENTATION

IN THE WORKS OF

FREDERICK CHOPIN

BY

JOHN PETRIE DUNN.

(LECTURER IN MUSIC AT THE UNIVERSITY OF EDINBURGH.)

LONDON: NOVELLO AND COMPANY, LIMITED.
NEW YORK: THE H. W. GRAY CO., SOLE AGENTS FOR THE U.S.A.
MADE IN ENGLAND.

PREFACE.

THE present book is an attempt to establish the correct pianistic treatment of the ornamentation in which Chopin's works are so rich. It is based, and could indeed be based only on internal evidence, for the traditional knowledge we possess regarding this aspect of Chopin's art is disappointingly vague, when we consider how many musicians of high rank, and how many accomplished amateurs Chopin numbered among his friends and pupils. As an instance of this, we might quote a sentence from the narrative of Mikuli given on p. 185, Vol. II. of the admirable biography by Professor Frederick Niecks :*

" . . . . . Shakes, which he generally began with the auxiliary note, had not so much to be played quick, as with great evenness."

Now, in the course of this book I have pointed out, firstly, that simple shakes are rare in Chopin's works ; secondly, that with a few almost self-evident exceptions, they must begin with the principal and not with the auxiliary note, else tautology or ugliness will result. So much for the trustworthiness of such traditions as we possess.

Although I have confined myself strictly to ornamentation as employed by Chopin, I venture to hope that the principles I have enunciated and followed will be of service to those desirous of investigating other composers' methods, no matter how much or how little the latter resemble those of the Polish master.

Embellishments, originally almost a spontaneous product of the short-lived tone of instruments whose strings are struck or plucked, and a veritable necessity to the composer who essayed to "set" for the pianoforte the long-drawn, emotional note of the human voice, gradually laid aside their makeshift, fortuitous character, and became the means whereby the composer could modify at will the expression and accentuation of his melodies, ranging, through many intermediate gradations, from outspoken bluntness to gentlest insinuation.

This development culminated in the works of Chopin. His ornamentation represents the high-water mark of the artistic *versus* the mechanical use of embellishments. It may be imitated, and—now that we understand his methods—might even be equalled. But it can never be excelled, for it is perfection itself.

JOHN PETRIE DUNN.

EDINBURGH, JUNE, 1921.

---

* "Frederick Chopin as a Man and Musician," Novello and Co., London.

DEFINITIONS.

1. AN ornament consists of one or more "grace notes" following, or followed by a "principal note". Thus, in the "Transient Shake":—

the first two notes (C, D) are grace notes, the third (C) is the principal note. In the "Turn":—

the first (C) is the principal note, the remaining notes of the quintolet are grace notes.

2. An ornament can either be played "on the beat", or "anticipated" (played before the beat). When, for example, in the following figure:—

we play the transient shake "on the beat" (as in Chopin's works we almost invariably should), its execution is as follows:—

The value of the first two notes of the ᴧᴠ is deducted from that of the principal note C, and the first of the demisemiquavers falls on the first beat of the bar and shares to a certain extent in the accent.

If, on the other hand, we "anticipate" the ᴧᴠ, its execution will assume the following form:—

This differs radically from the other, in that the time value of the first two notes of the ᴧᴠ is now deducted, not from the principal note C, but from the note immediately before it.

This distinction, as we shall presently see, is one of extreme importance.

PART I.

THE ORNAMENTS USED BY CHOPIN.

CHAPTER I.

THE SIMPLE SHAKE.

Notation :

Execution :

The simple shake is comparatively rare in Chopin's works. *When no direction to the contrary is given, it should invariably begin with the principal note.* If Chopin wishes it to commence with the auxiliary note, he prefixes the latter as an acciaccatura :—

Note, in addition, the meaning of the following notation :

The effect of the shake is to enliven or electrify the note over which it is placed.

When Chopin wishes the shake to conclude with a turn, he is most particular to indicate this in the usual way :—

When he omits the turn, the player is intended to lead straight on to the next note :—

CHAPTER II.

THE TRANSIENT SHAKE.

Notation :

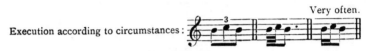

Execution according to circumstances :

The transient shake is one of Chopin's favourite embellishments. It almost always begins on the beat and is not anticipated :—

1. RONDEAU À LA MAZUR, Op. 5.

Execution :

Bass note.   Bass note.

2. WALTZ, Op. 34, No. 2.

Execution :

In rapid movement, the transient shake enlivens or accentuates the note to which it is attached. But in slow movement, more especially in *piano* and *pianissimo*, its gentle dalliance tends rather to soften the blow of the principal note. Here we catch our first glimpse of the important truth that *the effect of an embellishment varies according to the tempo and the character of its context.*

ACCENTUATION. Most players accentuate the third note of the transient shake. This is usually unnecessary, for if the *tempo* is sufficiently slow to admit of the subdivision ♪♪ or ♪♪ , the longest note (the last) will sound as if it were accentuated. The passage last quoted is an example of this.

If, on the other hand, the rapidity of the *tempo* obliges the player to execute the transient shake as a triplet, the accent will fall naturally on the note to which it belongs, *viz.* the first. Here, for example :—

3. NOCTURNE, Op. 32, No. 2, middle movement.

the player should perform every shake without exception as a triplet :—

Any attempt to accentuate the third note is musically uncalled for and technically precarious.

The rule may therefore be laid down that if the player executes the transient shake in accordance with the rhythmical subdivision which his musical judgment has impelled him to select, the right accentuation will follow as a matter of course.

CHAPTER III.

THE SHAKE FROM BELOW.

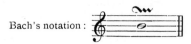

Bach's notation :

Chopin's notation :

Occasionally.

Execution :

or

This ornament, an especial favourite with Chopin, is usually played quite wrongly. Note therefore the following facts concerning it :—

It is not anticipated. The first of the grace notes falls on the beat of the principal note, and the time value of the grace notes is accordingly deducted from that of the principal note. The following example will make this clear :

4. BALLADE, Op. 47.

Execution :

(The accent in the right hand indicates a slight raising of the .
G flat above the tone level of the surrounding notes.)

Generally speaking, the function of the shake from below is to
insinuate the principal note (G flat in the above example), in
preference to enunciating it boldly. It approaches the latter in
a roundabout way, delays it somewhat, and makes its entry less
conspicuous. This, as we shall see later on, is the explanation
of Chopin's fondness for it.

The first of the grace notes frequently collides with the
accompanying harmony, *e.g.*—

5. SCHERZO, Op. 39.

6. BALLADE, Op. 38.

In these wild and gloomy passages, the momentary clash is merely a drop in the tempestuous ocean of sound, and the player must on no account seek to elude the "dissonance" by playing the grace notes before the beat, for the dissonance is intentional.

The accentuation of the shake from below varies with the context. In this grave, sweet phrase:

7. NOCTURNE, Op. 32, No. 2.

Execution of shake:

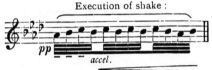

the shake is the starting point of a little climax that culminates in the A flat of the next bar; begin it very softly, then make a gradual *crescendo*, emphasizing the principal note (B flat) once or twice very slightly.

In vigorous passages, the grace notes should often be as strongly marked as the principal note; the above extracts from the Scherzo and the Ballade exemplify this. Another example is the following:—

8. SONATA, Op. 58, first movement.

All the grace-notes, as well as the shake, should be played with full, contralto tone.

In the following passage, however:

9. NOCTURNE, Op. 48, No. 2.

the player will do well to make the principal note swell out a little—

in order that the expressive interval

may not be swallowed up by the surrounding haze of tone.

CHAPTER IV.

THE TURN.

Form (*a*) is scarcely ever employed by Chopin. For an example, *v.* POLONAISE, Op. 71, No. 3, bars 23 and 24.

Form (*b*) occurs most frequently in the Nocturnes, more rarely in the Impromptus and Ballades, very rarely in the other works.

Chopin is wont to ornament the turn by prefixing one or two appoggiaturas to it. Of this, more anon.

Chopin's turns all possess melodic significance. They should be played very distinctly, even in the softest passages.

CHAPTER V.

THE INVERTED TURN.

A SPECIAL sign for this ornament—an inverted ∾ —was employed by C. P. E. Bach and Hummel,* but fell into disuse, as it was too easily mistaken for the ordinary turn.

Chopin writes it out in grace notes:

10. NOCTURNE, Op. 55, No. 2.

We play this as follows:—

In the one exceptional case we have been able to discover—

11. PRELUDE. Op. 28, No. 24.

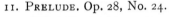

the grace notes are probably not an inverted turn at all, but an arbitrary ornament. With this one exception, all the inverted turns in Chopin should, in our opinion, be played on the beat.

The effect of this fine ornament is to enhance the poignancy of the principal note. It does not, however, lend itself to frequent employment, hence its rather rare appearance. In the above Nocturne—"Threnody" were a more fitting title—it is admirably in keeping with its surroundings.

---

* v. Dannreuther, "Ornamentation," Part II, p. 51. Novello and Co., London.

CHAPTER VI.

THE SLIDE.

Execution.

This ornament is not anticipated; the first of the grace notes falls on the beat.

12. MAZURKA, Op. 17, No. 2.

p dolce.

Execution of the slide :

Anticipation—

would result in an ornament worthier of the bagpipe than of the pianoforte.

Hearken, again, to the anticipation of the slide in the double-bass refrain of the MAZURKA, Op. 6, No 3 :

13

How coarse and snarling it sounds !

In regard to the effect of the slide, it will be found that the grace notes are more pronouncedly integral to the melody than in most other embellishments, and it is matter for debate whether Chopin would not have done better to incorporate them in the text in notes of normal size.

As regards the accentuation of the slide, we refer the reader to what was said in Chapter II. concerning the accentuation of the transient shake. Inelegance in the execution of Chopin's ornaments is very frequently due to the desire at all costs to emphasize the principal note.

CHAPTER VII.

THE ACCIACCATURA AND APPOGGIATURA.

14. In the opening bars of the POLONAISE, Op. 26, No. 1, Chopin writes out the acciaccatura :

The little crescendo marks are intended to warn the player not to over-emphasize the demisemiquavers.

The execution and effect of these ornaments vary so greatly in detail that we prefer to relegate their discussion to a later chapter.

CHAPTER V.II.

THE DOUBLE APPOGGIATURA.

This is the ornament which C. P. E. Bach terms the "Anschlag". It is played on the beat. In the following passage from the Rondo, Op. 16:—

15.

it should be subdivided thus :—

The demisemiquavers must be played with the greatest lightness and speed.

16. The middle section of the Polonaise, Op. 44, contains many examples of the double appoggiatura, all played in the same way :—

The effect of the double appoggiatura is similar to that of the appoggiatura and transient shake. It is a simple, easy ornament and calls for no further exemplification.

Accentuation. Strive after clearness and rapidity and leave the accentuation to settle itself.

CHAPTER IX.

THE ARPEGGIO.

Notation :

Chopin very often employs the more elaborate form :

EXECUTION AND EFFECT.

(*a*) *The Arpeggio in the right hand alone* always begins on the beat.

17. NOCTURNE, Op. 62, No. 1, bars 7—9.

(*b*) *The Arpeggio in the left hand alone* is generally anticipated, because if played on the beat it would hamper and retard the right hand and might give rise to crude effects of harmony. But the anticipation need only be slight. Here, for example :—

18. MAZURKA, Op. 7, No. 3.

the lowest note of each arpeggio is anticipated a little, the next
(C) coincides with the melody note of the right hand, and the
highest (A flat) follows immediately in its train. The three notes
must follow one another in quickest succession, otherwise they
will produce a drawling, dragging effect.

Further on, we encounter the passage :—

(Outline.)

Here, it is not essential that the topmost note in the left hand
(F) should synchronize with the chord in the right. It may come
after it a little and yet arrive quite soon enough to complete the
harmony and satisfy the ear.

(c) *The distribution of arpeggios occurring simultaneously in
both hands* varies according to circumstances and demands much
taste and discrimination. Now the arpeggios begin and end
together (ETUDE, Op. 10, No. 11, throughout) ; now the right
hand enters when the left has finished (ETUDE, Op. 25, No. 6,
penultimate chord) ; often, the right hand allows the left to play
one or two notes in advance, *e.g.*

19. ETUDE, Op. 25, No. 4.

In the first chord, play the grace note D (R.H.) together with the F of the left hand; in the concluding chord, the C sharp coincides with the topmost A of the left hand :—

The following generalization may be useful :—

Why is (3) the least satisfactory way of playing the arpeggio? Because the right hand doubles three of the bass notes in the octave, and this gives them an unnatural prominence. If then, any rule can be formulated with regard to the distribution of arpeggios, it is this : *avoid consecutive octaves.* And should the reader desire confirmation of the rule, let him examine the ETUDE, Op. 10, No. 11,—the apotheosis of the appeggio. He will find that of the three hundred odd chords composing it, some twenty only are so set as to make octave doubling practically unavoidable.

The effect produced by the arpeggio varies according to the *tempo,* instrumentation, character, and degree of loudness or softness of the context. Obviously, one of its principal uses is to co-operate with the pedal in building up chords the intervals of which are too wide to admit of their being sounded simultaneously. Again, a chord often gains surprisingly in expressive force, or fits more smoothly into its surroundings by being arpeggioed.

In gentle melodies, the arpeggio softens the rhythmical impact of the principal note, but renders the latter more audible by making it follow in the train of all the other notes. In *forte* and *fortissimo,* again, it imparts a certain grandiloquence to the outstanding notes of impassioned themes. Many an instance of this will be found in the ALLEGRO DE CONCERT, Op. 46, a work almost unsurpassed in splendour of tone colour and instrumentation.

CHAPTER X.

THE SLOW TREMOLO.

THIS is the " Bebung " of C. P. E. Bach and consists of the expressive *legatissimo* reiteration of one note (generally *cres.* or *dim.*). Chopin indicates it by a slur :

20. ETUDE, Op. 25, No. 2, end.

If possible, the finger should hold the key slightly below its high level in order to soften the blow of the hammer by shortening its journey; the tone resulting from this—subdued, almost stifled—being admirably adapted to clavichord-like repercussions or echoes. It is, however, but fair to say that one seldom has time to avail oneself of this delicate style of touch.

Chopin employs the Bebung fairly often,—generally for a few notes only at a time ; he always draws attention to it by slurring the repeated notes.

CONCLUSION OF PART I.

THE MORDENT.

OF the ornaments frequently used by the older composers, one is conspicuous by its absence in the pages of Chopin. It is the Mordent :—

We may find a partial explanation of this curious fact in an idiosyncrasy that reveals itself repeatedly in Chopin's melodies, more especially in the opening bars of his themes. Let the reader compare the following extracts, chosen at random from the countless instances available :—

WALTZ, Op. 72.

It will be seen that the above beginnings of phrases are based on the patterns ⌐‾‾‾⌐ or ⌐‾‾‾⌐ Instances of the converse pattern occur, but they are much rarer. It would appear, therefore, that Chopin's primary melodic bias—his shibboleth, so to speak—were an ascending, followed by a descending oscillation of the melodic line. Hence his predilection for the Transient Shake, and his total neglect of its counterpart, the Mordent.

MISCELLANEOUS EMBELLISHMENTS.

In addition to the embellishments enumerated in the foregoing chapters, Chopin employs a number of cadenzas and ornaments constructed either arbitrarily or by the combination of two of the standard embellishments, as for instance: Appoggiatura + Turn, repeated Appoggiatura + Arpeggio, etc. A number of these will be considered as they arise; in the meantime, it will suffice to to say that the execution of the composite ornaments will present little or no difficulty to anyone who has grasped the principles underlying Chopin's methods of embellishment. This will be made additionally clear in the following chapters.

PART II.

CHOPIN'S METHODS OF ORNAMENTATION.
EXAMPLES AND DETAILS.

CHAPTER XI.

CHARACTERISTICS OF CHOPIN'S STYLE.

A few general remarks on Chopin's ornamentation may not be out of place here.

Note, firstly, Chopin's fondness for devious melodic routes and his dislike of abruptness and angularity. Where others would write:

21. SONATA, Op. 35, Funeral March.

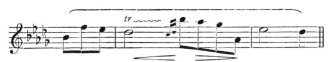

Chopin dallies with the outstanding notes of the melody, quits them reluctantly, and masks the entry of each:

The arpeggio and appoggiatura are repeatedly employed by him in this way.

It is clear that the vast majority of Chopin's embellishments should begin on the beat, for by anticipating them, we frustrate Chopin's object in employing them. If in the above extract, for example, the ornaments were anticipated:—

the triplets, so far from softening the blow of the principal notes, would have exactly the opposite effect.

Ornamentation is much more essential to the pianoforte than to other instruments. A violin or clarinet can produce a beautiful effect in the following way :—

The pianoforte cannot do so, but Chopin has standardized the methods by which such effects can at least be suggested.

It is further characteristic of Chopin's fondness for gliding movement that when passing from one octave to the next, he does not leap boldly as other composers do, but builds a ladder or staircase of tones to make the ascent or descent easier. Moreover, he often contrives at the same time to suggest the entry of fresh voices or instruments, translating orchestral effects into the language of the pianoforte in the following way :—

22. NOCTURNE, Op. 48, No. 2.   N.B.

Here we have to understand the chord at N.B. as the octave doubling of the lower voices by a fresh group of instruments. We must accordingly give the grace notes at N.B. their due weight, for if we hasten over them perfunctorily in order to reach the top notes sooner, we brush aside as unessential the harmonic substratum represented by them :

But the latter is, for the moment, even more important that the doubling in the higher octave, for it is the medium by which the composer is enabled to *suggest* what the player's fingers cannot literally accomplish, *viz.* the continuous doubling of the lower voices for five bars on end:

&c.

Observe, too, that Chopin greatly widens the spacing of the left hand arpeggios in order to heighten the suggestion of middle voices.

The right effect of the passage, then, is contingent on the non-anticipation of the grace notes, and we must consequently play them as follows :—

Ped.

23. The same applies to the third theme in the BALLADE Op. 47 :

Bass note
A♭.

Bass note
A♭.

The first of the grace notes must invariably fall on the beat
and coincide with the bass note.   We have to imagine the
junction between the second and third bars as follows:

But the usefulness of these connecting links in arpeggio or
other form does not end here, for in addition to bridging over
the gap between one octave and another, they enhance the
importance of the note to which they are leading.   The player
must, as it were, overcome their inertia before he can advance,
and he is accordingly compelled to tarry a little over that
particular portion of the bar.   Chopin in fact writes:

or the like, when another composer would be content with:

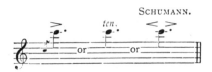

Chopin is thoroughly alive to the lack of sustaining power
inherent in the pianoforte; by a masterly use of ornamentation,
however, he beguiles the listener into the belief that the sustaining power is much greater than is actually the case.   He never
resorts to absurdly long *tenutos*, extravagant pedalling (Debussy!),
or impossible (because purely optical) crescendos on single notes.

Here we have another instance of that perfect adaptation of the means to the end that furnishes so clear a proof of the sanity of Chopin's genius.

Lastly, it remains to speak of the relation of Chopin's ornamentation to the *tempo rubato*. We shall very often find that the slight delay incidental to the execution of an ornament suggests the correct *rubato* delivery. In particular : a highly ornamented note often points out to us the climax, or slowest phase of the *rubato* :—

24. MAZURKA, Op. 7, No. 1.

A good player would in any case be tempted to linger slightly over the second bar of this passage, ornaments or no ornaments. The difficult composite embellishment (a transient shake beginning exceptionally with the auxiliary note) makes it impossible for him not to do so.

25. The NOCTURNE, Op. 48, No. 2, supplies us with another fine instance :

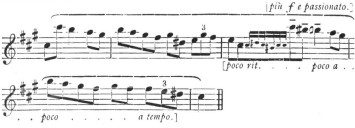

The ornament here symbolizes the intensified declamatory ardour which the player ought to impart to the repetition of the phrase.

The ornament—a turn + two appoggiaturas is difficult
to play neatly. It should be subdivided between the first and
second beats of the bar :

(Very light, rapid
and even.)

The following phrase, in Chopin's most grandiloquent manner,
is more and more lavishly ornamented as it rises to the
impassioned climax from which it hurls itself downward in a
cascade of octaves :

26. ALLEGRO DE CONCERT, Op. 46.

We shall therefore play the third bar *allargando*, dwell on the
topmost D sharp, and then proceed *accelerando*.

In such cases, the *ritenuto* or *allargando* might be likened
to the swelling of a river ; the *accelerando* to the opening of the
sluice-gates.

To sum up: Chopin very often compensates for a loss of
speed by giving the player more notes to perform, thus making
it " worth his while ", as it were, to linger over the retarded
episode. The moral of which is that we must read between the

lines for possibilities of *rubato* when Chopin suddenly or
gradually adds to the number of his embellishments.

In conclusion, let us state the main pianistic rules for the
execution of ornaments :

(1) Fix the fingering, using a change of fingers—*e.g.*

—whenever you think it necessary, but avoiding com-
plicated fingerings that are difficult to remember.

(2) Fix the rhythmical position of every note.

(3) Practise, at first rather emphatically, until you are quite
familiar with the " feel " of the passage.

(4) Play *musically*, and (in slow tempi) *vocally*. Never hurry
or blur an ornament. Strive after perfect distinctness,
even in the softest *pianissimo*.

(5) Lift your foot from the pedal when playing transient
shakes, turns, slides, and the like in the middle and
lower octaves of the pianoforte.

CHAPTER XII.

ADDITIONAL REMARKS ON THE SIMPLE SHAKE.*

THE shake presents very little difficulty. Chopin frequently
indicates the note with which it should commence, and the
shakes for which he has given no directions at all are relatively
few in number. As to the latter, it will be found on examining
them that they should all begin with the principal note, albeit
there are some which, without detriment to the melodic line,
might begin with the auxiliary note.

And now it may be asked : why does Chopin indicate the
initial note of the shake in some cases and not in others ? The

* This and the following chapters should be read in conjunction with the
corresponding chapters of Part I.

reason is simple: *Chopin indicates the initial note in order to leave no doubt whatever as to the right execution of shakes which, if commenced wrongly, would produce an exceptionally bad effect.*

Listen, for example, to the following tautology :— .

with its wearisome harping on the A sharp. The tautology, however, is merely the result of commencing the shake (the demisemiquavers) with the auxiliary note. Chopin foresaw this danger, and that is why he wrote the above passage as follows :—

27. SONATA, Op. 58, first movement.

28. Another example. In the MAZURKA, Op. 30, No. 4, bar 39 :

the shake *must* begin with G sharp, because A sharp would sound like a wrong note. The explanation of this is that during the preceding 38 bars the ear has become so acclimatized to the tonality of C sharp minor that the sudden entrance of the A sharp would give it a painful shock. Here again, Chopin has forestalled the danger.

In conclusion, we quote three passages that are often misread by students.

29. NOCTURNE, Op. 62, No. 1, bars 6—7 of the *Poco più lento.*

The second bar must begin with an unmistakable G natural; the reason is obvious.

The chain of shakes in bars 1—2 of the same passage should be played as follows:—

30. NOCTURNE, Op. 72, No. 1, bars 36—37.

Begin this shake with D; it is really a shake from below, anticipated.

---

* We have written out the little cadenza in large notes, in order to show the exact time-value of the notes composing it.

CHAPTER XIII.

EXAMPLES OF THE TRANSIENT SHAKE.

(a) *Anticipation of the Transient shake.*

VERY occasionally, the anticipation of the transient shake is either desirable or unavoidable. The characteristic properties of the transient shake, as described in the foregoing, make themselves felt most strongly when the latter is preceded by one or more notes. When therefore a transient shake stands over the first note of a phrase ; in particular : when it is preceded by a pause and not by a note whose time value would be lessened by its anticipation, the transient shake may sometimes be played before the beat without serious detriment to the melodic effect. In the following passages, for instance :—

31. WALTZ, Op. 34, No. 3.

32. IMPROMPTU, Op. 29.

it would not be unlawful to anticipate the first two notes of the shake. All the subsequent shakes in the Impromptu must however be played on the beat.

The transient shakes in the NOCTURNES, Op. 37, No. 2, and Op. 72, No. 1 (from bar 32 onwards) should be anticipated.

33. PRELUDE, Op. 28, No. 3, bar 17.

Undoubtedly an anticipation :

34. Compare with this bar 6 of the 21st PRELUDE :

The use of the notation  to denote an anticipated transient shake is however very rare. In the following passages —only a few from the many that offered themselves—the ornament is undoubtedly a transient shake proper, for its anticipation would produce a very bad effect :

35. BALLADE, Op. 23.

36. MAZURKA, Op. 33, No. 2.

37. CONCERTO, Op. 11, finale.

(b) *Miscellaneous Examples.*

38. WALTZ, Op. 64, No. 1.

The orthodox version of this is unplayable :—

We therefore advise the player to substitute an acciaccatura for the transient shake:—

39. WALTZ, Op. 34, No. 1.

Chopin's alternative notation for this is :

Same piece, bars 68—69.   Execution :—

or better :

egualmente.

40. In the WALTZ, Op. 34, No. 2, Chopin writes out the transient shake :

41. Play in the very same way the following bar from the WALTZ, Op. 64, No. 1 :

42. Very difficult to execute neatly is bar 14 of the *Meno mosso* of the POLONAISE, Op. 26, No. 1.   The transient shake must be subdivided in the normal way :—

Note, however, that the whole bar should be played *rallentando*, following the *stretto* (not indicated but doubtless intended by Chopin) of the preceding bars.

CHAPTER XIV.

THE " SHAKE FROM FELOW ".

OF the countless examples of this ornament we quote only the
following.   They all exhibit points of interest and furnish
confirmation of the rule that the shake from below must begin
on the beat.

43. NOCTURNE, Op. 15, No. 2.

Amateur pianists almost invariably botch this delicate little
bar of music, although there is scarcely a passage in all Chopin
in which the anticipation of an ornament has a worse effect.
Play it therefore as follows :

and enjoy for once the piquant effect of the harmony

$$\begin{cases} Fx \\ F\sharp \\ B\sharp \\ C\sharp \end{cases}$$

Less objectionable but nevertheless incorrect would be the
anticipation of the grace notes here :

44. IMPROMPTU, Op. 36.

Observe the parallelism of this and the previous version of the phrase :

45. BALLADE, Op. 23.

A beautiful example of musical logic, when correctly played. The first grace note must fall on the beat, together with the G of the right hand, otherwise the first four notes of the shake (D♯, E, F, E) will be out of keeping with the four quavers in the first half of the bar.

46. Precisely analogous is the shake leading to the final return to the key of F sharp major in the BARCAROLLE, Op. 60. Play the second half of the bar as follows :—

The effect of the following shake :

47. SONATA, Op. 35, *Scherzo*.

is harmonically very beautiful, provided the grace note D♮ be not anticipated but made to synchronize with the G♭ of the right hand.

48. PRELUDE, Op. 28, No. 24.

Bar 10 should be played thus :—

49. NOCTURNE, Op. 32, No. 2, the 5th bar before the end.

We now pass to the consideration of the only doubtful cases we have been able to discover.

50. SONATA IN B MINOR, Op. 58, first movement, the 15th bar after the final change to B major.

The collision of B♮ with B♯ is very harsh, and for this reason we would advise the player to depart from the rule and anticipate the first two grace notes :—

51. IMPROMPTU, Op. 29, middle section.

Did Chopin intend the anticipation of the first two grace
notes (G, A) in the following passage?—

We almost think so, for they would then correspond neatly to
the last notes of the bar (G♯, A) as well as to the last notes of
the preceding bar (F, G). Melodically, the anticipation of the
two notes is more logical than their inclusion in the beat of the
principal note, and this is felt even more strongly when we play
the passage than when we merely follow the melodic outline
with the eye. Let us, however, forbear to draw any conclusions
from the passage and agree to regard it as an exception to an
almost invariable rule.

52. PRELUDE, Op. 28, No. 23.

The very difficult ornament—

ought to be played in this way:—

But it is almost impossible to get all the notes in, unless we
adopt an unnaturally slow *tempo* for the entire piece. The fact
is that the grace notes themselves consume almost all the time
available for the shake. We think therefore that it would be
permissible either to anticipate the first two grace notes, or to
play simply as follows:

—a version which does justice to the spirit, if not to the letter
of Chopin's text.

CHAPTER XV.

ADDITIONAL EXAMPLES OF THE TURN.

CERTAIN passages, in which Chopin has written out the turn in full, throw light on his manner of performing it. A quintolet would appear to be his favourite rhythmical subdivision:

53. NOCTURNE, Op. 27, No. 1.

54. NOCTURNE, Op. 32, No. 1.

See also the NOCTURNES, Op. 27, No. 2, bar 16, and Op. 32, No. 2, bar 9.

Suggestive, too, is the following passage:—

55. ETUDE, Op. 25, No. 7.

where the five notes (marked *N.B.*) resemble a turn in the form of a quintolet with the first note slightly lengthened. Chopin might possibly have written it thus:—

had he not feared that this notation might tempt the performer to execute it as rapidly as the corresponding turn two bars earlier :

Retaining in our mind the explicit notation of the above passages, let us now review a number of turns written in a more ambiguous way.

56. NOCTURNE, Op. 15, No. 1.

As with many other quintolet turns, the first note (G) should receive a slight stress.

Compare with this the FANTAISIE - IMPROMPTU, Op. 66, *Moderato cantabile*, bar 11, and the PRELUDE in E minor, Op. 28, No. 4, bar 16.

57. NOCTURNE, Op. 37, No. 1.

In example (*b*), version (1) is quite correct, but we give the preference to version (2), as being the more Chopinesque. If (2) be adopted, the player should dwell perceptibly on the first C, slightly on the second, scarcely at all on the third. The three C's then form a "Slow Tremolo" ("Bebung"), and the entire group of notes (marked "*rubato*") is enlivened by a delicate *accelerando*. Save by a crabbed notation, the time value of the notes of a passage like this could not be indicated precisely on paper, and this is one of the reasons why Chopin writes them as grace notes.

58. NOCTURNE, Op. 48, No. 1.

Execution of the turn :

The quintolet should be played with a certain deliberation, for it is the end of a *ritenuto* leading back to the original *tempo* after the *accelerando* of the preceding bars.

59. NOCTURNE, Op. 62, No. 1, bar 12. Execution of the turn :—

A quintolet would here sound too drawling.

60. IMPROMPTU, Op. 29.

This is a composite embellishment : *Bebung* plus Turn. Dwell on the first two or three notes, then make a gentle *accelerando*.

The continuation three bars further on should be played as follows :

61. PRELUDE, Op. 28, No. 15, bar 11 :—

So also bars 15 and 17.

62. SONATA, Op. 58, *Largo* (6 bars before the end). Play the composite turn thus :—

CHAPTER XVI.

EXAMPLES OF THE SLIDE.

63. POLONAISE, Op. 71, No. 3 (second part).

If the reader will examine the context, he will see now ingeniously the slide is here employed to connect this bar with the preceding one. The above bar is the first of the after-phrase and is a variation of the first bar of the fore-phrase :—

It must therefore begin with E♭. But Chopin, true to his principles, cannot write

 &c.

His sensitive ear rejects this as too crude, too primitive, and he
therefore carries the D♭ smoothly downward to C and thence,
by his favourite circuitous route, upwards through D♭ to the
final destination E♭.   Nothing could be more tasteful or more
logical.

The passage should be played thus : —

64. ETUDE, Op. 10, No. 3, the bar before the *Poco più
animato*.

This case is interesting in another way.   The various editions
differ in their reading of the bar.   In the very important reprint
by Professor Rudorff,* based on Chopin's autographs and the
original editions, we find

Others have

All these readings give a good sense, but they are not equally
Chopinesque.   If the reader endorses what was said in the
foregoing chapters regarding Chopin's methods of ornamentation,
he will give the preference to the first version and will play as
follows :—

---

* *Urtext Classischer Musikwerke*, Breitkopf and Härtel, Leipzig.

A Caution to the Student.

Chopin sometimes writes certain conventional turns of melody or delicate connecting notes as grace notes, leaving it to the player to time them correctly. Thus, in the POLONAISE, Op. 26, No. 1, *Meno mosso*, bar 4, he writes

65.

and in the CONCERTO, Op. 21, near the beginning of the development section of the first movement :

66.

The grace notes here do not constitute a slide, nor have they—except on paper—any resemblance to one. They are anticipated, whereas the outstanding mark of a slide is that its first note falls on the beat.

67. POLONAISE, Op. 71, No. 2.

Here it is obvious that Chopin means

but refrained from writing so, in order to avoid the accumulation of cross-strokes. Three bars later, we find

This, on the other hand, is undoubtedly a slide.

CHAPTER XVII.

ACCIACCATURA AND APPOGGIATURA.

THE ornaments of this class may be divided into three categories:—(1) The *Acciaccatura*, or the very light and quick appoggiatura. Normally, it falls on the beat, but as it comes and goes in a flash, the ear cannot in rapid *tempi* determine its exact rhythmical position. Examples will be found in the WALZES, Op. 18 and Op. 34, No. 3.

The acciaccatura requires no further discussion.

(2) The *Appoggiatura*, which falls on the beat and is now short and subdued, now long and accentuated.

(3) The *Anticipation*, or appoggiatura played in advance of the beat.

(a) *The Appoggiatura.*

Chopin habitually employs the appoggiatura to indicate the soft, rapid breaking of an octave or chord of two notes. Cases like the following :

68. MAZURKA, Op 17, No. 4.

are numberless and should always be treated in the same way,— the appoggiatura on the beat, slightly masking and delaying the principal note.

Often, the appoggiatura is repeated :

69. POLONAISE, Op. 53.

This is identical with

and its execution is

The appoggiaturas here thicken and emphasize the octave.

Sometimes, however, the appoggiatura masks the entry of the principal note to such an extent as to usurp its place :—

70. CONCERTO, Op. 11, finale.

71. MAZURKA, Op. 33, No. 4.

The appoggiaturas marked *N.B.* are not genuine ornaments at all, but are integral to the melody, as is felt at once when they are omitted. Play, for example, the two bars of the Mazurka, leaving out the appoggiatura; the result is nonsense. From this it follows that the appoggiaturas in those passages should be accentuated just as strongly as the principal notes.

It is quite impossible to formulate any rule that would enable the performer to determine the relative degree of emphasis or melodic importance to be assigned to each and every appoggiatura. He must judge every case on its own merits and be guided by his musical instincts, assisted by a wide acquaintanceship with the master's works.

Further examples:—

72. BALLADE, Op. 47.

(a)

(b)

The following case is doubtful:

73. POLONAISE-FANTAISIE, Op. 61.

The appoggiatura might be played as a crotchet, but we feel that it ought to be played as a quaver, although we can advance no argument in support of this.

74. SCHERZO, Op. 54.

With one exception, all the appoggiaturas in this work should fall on the beat, *e.g.*

Execution :

The one exception is the appoggiatura (plus arpeggio) in bar
89, which we think should be played thus:

75. ETUDE, Op. 25, No. 5.

Here Chopin has written out the appoggiatura, supplying us
with a model for all similar passages.

In bars 29—36, the appoggiaturas should be timed exactly as
in bars 1—20. The only difference between the two passages
is that in bars 29—36 the upper voice is *tenuto*, whereas in bars
1—20 it is *staccato* (♪♩ ♩ ♪♩ ♩ ♪♩ ♩).

Follow this pattern in the MAZURKA, Op. 6, No. 1, middle
section.

76. PRELUDE, Op. 28, No. 7.

Play the appoggiatura on the beat, together with the left hand
chord, and follow it up at once with the remaining notes C♯ and
A. (Change the pedal as indicated and do not attempt to
sustain the deep A through both bars.)

77. The BERCEUSE, Op. 57, contains some important instances. That the appoggiaturas in bars 15—18 should not be anticipated is clear from the analogy of bar 14 :

For similar reasons, we must play the appoggiatura at the beginning of bar 31 as follows: --

So also in the following :—

78. BARCAROLLE, Op. 60.

79. CONCERTO, Op. 11, first movement.

Execution approximately :

(b) *Anticipations.*

When the note following an appoggiatura is identical with the latter, the appoggiatura is anticipated.

Examples :—

80. NOCTURNE, Op. 32, No. 2.   Play bar 14 thus :—

(*Very delicately.*)

Chopin occasionally indicates this by slurring the appoggiatura
to the note that precedes it. *V.* the PRELUDE, Op. 28, No. 15,
bar 4; also the NOCTURNE, Op. 37, No. 1, bar 5, which should be
played thus :—

These are exceptional cases.   Normally, the appoggiatura in
a composite ornament falls on the beat.

The appoggiatura in bar 14 of the last-named piece should
likewise be anticipated :—

81. PRELUDE, Op. 28, No. 5.   The appoggiatura in the last
bar should be anticipated.

82. ETUDE, Op. 10, No. 5.

Execution :

CHAPTER XVIII.

EXAMPLES OF THE ARPEGGIO.

83. Mazurka, Op. 67, No. 1.

Observe that when the wavy line ⸾ extends unbrokenly from
from top to bottom of the stave, this does not necessarily imply
that the notes of the entire chord should follow one another
singly. In the last example, there would be no time to arpeggio
the chord in that way, even if it were desirable to do so.

84. Polonaise, Op. 26, No. 1.

This case is exactly similar to that which was discussed
under Example 18. The note C sharp is played just before
the beat; B is played *on* the beat together with E sharp of the
right hand; E sharp in the tenor brings up the rear. The slight
delay of the latter note, so far from being a blemish, has, we
think, a rhythmical charm of its own,—the charm of the
irregular.

To avoid tedious repetition, let us say once and for all, that this manner of playing left-hand arpeggios is generally the best. But observe, firstly, that it is applicable only to arpeggioed chords that accompany a single note or non-arpeggioed chord in the right hand; secondly, that it does not constitute an invariable rule. The player is free to perform the arpeggio on the beat or to anticipate one or all of its notes, as the case may be. Here, for example:—

85. NOCTURNE, Op. 15, No. 1.

the first of the two arpeggios may be played either on the beat or in the manner described above; the second arpeggio ought certainly to begin on the beat (as shewn in margin), if only in order to avoid mishaps with the pedal.

86. NOCTURNE, Op. 32, No. 1.

87. NOCTURNE, Op. 48, No. 2.

Here it is best to anticipate the low D flat.

88. Nocturne, Op. 48, No. 1, middle movement. (The large notes are those which should fall on the beat; the others are played either before or after the beat, as indicated.)

89. Nocturne, Op. 62, No. 1, 16 bars before the end. The broken chord should be played thus:

It has the force of a stress ($\mathrel{\raise1pt\hbox{$\scriptstyle\searrow$}}$).

90. IMPROMPTU, Op. 29, nine bars before the end:

91. FANTAISIE-IMPROMPTU, Op. 66.   The concluding chords
should be arpeggioed successively :—

92. In the concluding section of the SCHERZO, Op. 54, the
arpeggios all fall on the beat, *e.g.*—

93. In the ETUDE, Op. 10, No. 11, the arpeggios should begin
and end simultaneously in the right and left hand:

94. ETUDE, Op. 25, No. 1, last bar.

Play the E flat of the left hand with the C of the right. Or, still better, play as follows :—

Generally speaking, an arpeggio sounds more elegant when the right hand has more notes to play than the left.

95. ETUDE, Op. 25, No. 2, concluding bars.

Penultimate bar : subdivide the grace-notes thus :—

[*slowly.*]

Last bar : play the five notes one after the other rather rapidly and very softly.

96. ETUDE, Op. 25, No. 5, the difficult three bars preceding the *Più lento*, and the corresponding passage near the end. Pattern :—

Play the grace-notes in the left hand with the utmost rapidity.

97. PRELUDE, Op. 28, No. 3.

In this piece, many an undignified scramble might be saved if players would refrain from attempting to crowd the notes of the arpeggios into the bars preceding them. Bar 18 is a case in point. Correctly interpreted, it runs smoothly and easily:—

98. PRELUDE, Op. 28, No. 8, last bar:

99. PRELUDE, Op. 28, No. 13, Part III. (*Tempo* 1), the passage beginning six bars before the end.

Play as follows:—

taking care to mark the notes of the melody (G♯, A♯, &c.). The highest notes are merely a faint reverberation of the latter.

This passage is instructive in another sense, as showing to what lengths Chopin is prepared to go in the mingling of harmonic with non-harmonic notes by means of the pedal.

100. SONATA, Op. 35, first movement (*Grave*), bar 3.

A fine example of declamatory emphasis supplied by the arpeggio. The first of the grace-notes coincides with the bass note F; dwell slightly upon it and accelerate the remainder, arriving *fortissimo* at the top note.

The bars following the change to B flat major should be
played thus :

In the first bar, the treble note F would be dulled and clouded
by contact with the F of the left hand ; it must stand out alone.

101. CONCERTO IN F MINOR, Op. 21, first movement, beginning
of development.

102. VARIATIONS ON "LÀ CI DAREM," Op. 2, Introduction.

All the charm of this passage would be lost if the arpeggios were
anticipated.   The delay of the principal notes, which float hazily
into their place in line, is certainly intentional and has a beautiful
effect.

The analogous passage three pages further on (" *staccato, ma
leggiero* ") should be played in exactly the same way ; no effort
need be made to edge in the grace notes—*e.g.* :—

—before the beat.

CHAPTER XIX.

ADDITIONAL REMARKS ON THE EXECUTION AND PEDALLING OF ARPEGGIOS.

PIANOFORTE students usually attempt to play big arpeggios in rapid movements more loudly than is physically possible, and this leads to " squelching," splashing, and indistinctness.   We take this opportunity, therefore, of pointing out that the wide sweep of an arpeggio in *forte* or *fortissimo* passages is in itself sufficient to produce the effect of loudness, provided that each note of the arpeggio be struck cleanly and distinctly.

103. In the 14th bar of the ETUDE, Op. 10, No. 8, for example :

do not try to play the very rapid grace notes as loudly as the semiquavers of the right hand ; their clear articulation is all that is required.

The reason why it is not possible to play rapid arpeggios *fortissimo* is that in executing them we are obliged to rely principally on the strength of the fingers.   Anything more than a very modest reinforcement of the latter by means of the weight or the downward pressure of the arm will glue the hand to the keys, with the " squelching " results aforesaid.

The pedalling of arpeggioed chords also require attention. The rule may be laid down that *the pedal should always be taken on the first note of the harmony that is sounded, no matter where that note may occur,—in bass, treble, or middle voice.*

Very frequent are cases like the following :

104. NOCTURNE, Op. 62, No. 1.

in which the grace note, being essential to the completeness of
the harmony, must not be suffered to drop out of sight but
must be caught up by the pedal.   This would have been more
clearly shown, if Chopin had written as follows :

Another example :

105. WALTZ in E minor.   (Posthumous work.)

Here we must beware of changing the pedal too late and thus
forfeiting the most important note G♯.

    More difficult to manage are passages containing notes which,
being foreign to the harmony, must *not* be prolonged by the
pedal, *e.g.*—

106. NOCTURNE, Op. 32, No. 2.

The quaver B♭ must be released immediately before playing the bass note A♭, for if the finger rests on the B♭ for the fraction of a second beyond the proper moment, the pedal will seize hold of that note and thrust it clashingly into the midst of the notes composing the A♭ triad. It may be objected that the release of the B♭ will cause a gap in the melody; the player need, however, have no anxiety on that account, for the gap is filled up by the intervening notes of the arpeggio.

In the important passage already quoted from the 13th Nocturne (Example 88), the player must be particularly careful to catch up the lowest note of each arpeggio with the pedal, at the same time removing his fingers from the keys which he has just been holding down.

CHAPTER XX.

THE SLOW TREMOLO OR BEBUNG.

THERE are a few passages in Chopin's works which, although not tremolos or *Bebungen* in the sense defined by us, are nevertheless akin to these.

Foremost amongst them stands the coda of the BERCEUSE, Op. 57:

107.

Latent or stationary voice.

Melody.

This passage, four bars long, is a lazy ebb and flow of the melodic tide past the stationary note C♭. Now and again, the latter shows its head above the surface; finally (at the resolution into B♭) it is submerged. In other words: whenever the melody crosses the stationary voice at the note C♭, the player must emphasise that note, causing it to *pervade* the entire melody from the beginning up to the long deferred resolution. At the notes marked with an accent, the emphasis must be fervent but not violent; elsewhere it should be very gentle.

108. In the POLONAISE, Op. 26, No. 1, we encounter the same effect on a microscopic scale :—

To bring out the warbling effect of it, we may conceive the passage as follows:

and touch in the acciaccaturas with the most delicate of strokes.

For another precisely similar passage, consult the POLONAISE, Op. 53, the fourteenth bar after the double bar marking the return from E to A♭ major.

CHAPTER XXI.

ARBITRARY ORNAMENTS AND CADENZAS.

WHEN the conventional ornaments occurring in Chopin's works have been elucidated, few difficulties relating to this aspect of his music remain to harass the student. The arbitrary ornaments, and more particularly the " cadenzas "—those flocks of notes that circle in the musical ether, far above the harmony from which they took their flight—will prove quite amenable to law and order when once we have familiarized ourselves with certain singularities of Chopin's style and notation.

The student of Chopin's works must often have asked himself the question : why has Chopin so frequently employed minute notes of conventional time-value to express what might have been noted much more unequivocally in the usual way? Why, for example does he write

109. NOCTURNE, Op. 37, No. 1.

instead of

There are several answers to this question ; we give them in order of importance.

Firstly, Chopin's musical upbringing, in which the works of the older composers had bulked very largely, favoured the use of conventional signs.

Secondly, Chopin's refined sense of order led him to consider the optical as well as the aural effect of his music. Tangles of 32nd and 64th notes offend his eye. He therefore divides the notes of his melodies into two classes : (1) the principal (those forming the framework) and (2) the accessory (the ornaments and the more fugitive of the connecting notes). The former he writes in large characters, the latter in small, and thus expresses optically his sense of their relative importance. Cadenzas occur in his works, the notes of which are plainly meant to be apportioned in equal numbers to those of the accompaniment, and which might conveniently have been written in the ordinary

way.   Even for those, Chopin uses minuscule type, as a symbol
of their subordinate rank.   This practice leads at times to a
certain ambiguity, but this disadvantage is outweighed by the
resulting beautiful perspicuousness.   Such transparent clearness
amidst picturesque luxuriance has no parallel in music.

Thirdly, Chopin's notation reacts on our playing.   We tend
instinctively to touch in the accessory detail with a lighter hand
when it is presented to our eye in its characteristic diamond
type.   Can there be any doubt that Chopin intended this ?

Fourthly, and most important of all, it would have been
impossible for Chopin, even by a meticulous system of notation,
to record those minute *rubato* inflections, those microscopic
lengthenings and shortenings of notes, and quickenings and
slackenings of the speed that are essential to the interpretation of
every page of his works.   Printed type can do no more than
suggest them ; their detailed interpretation must be left to the
taste and discretion of the player.

*   *   *   *

We now pass to a review of a number of Chopin's cadenzas.
Let it be said at the outset that our directions concerning their
performance are not absolutely binding, but are intended rather
to serve merely as a guide to less experienced players.   To lay
down hard and fast rules would be inconsistent with what we
have said above regarding the rhythmical latitude demanded by
Chopin's style.   To economize space, we shall write out only
such cadenzas as cannot be elucidated otherwise ; for the
the remainder, an indication of their arithmetical subdivision
will suffice.   When, for example, we say that a cadenza should
be apportioned thus : $6+6+6+5$, we mean that it should be
subdivided into four groups comprising 6, 6, 6, and 5 notes
respectively, and that the first note of each group must coincide
with the corresponding accompanimental note, *e.g.*—

110. IMPROMPTU, Op. 36.

We shall exclude from our discussion all cadenzas whose subdivision is obvious, such as the cadenza of 24 notes in the F major section of the above IMPROMPTU.

*   *   *   *

111. POLONAISE, Op. 53, eight bars after "*sostenuto*".

112. POLONAISE-FANTAISIE, Op. 61, bar 1 *seqq*.

Directions for performance: (1) No accentuation whatever. (The bar lines are added merely as a guide to the eye.) (2) Play *rubato, i.e., ritenuto—accelerando—ritenuto.* (3) *Tempo* as in bar 1. (4) Begin *piano*, make a slight *crescendo*, and then die away towards the close. The passage must sound mysterious and oracular.

(The other cadenzas should be arranged on some similar plan.)

Ibid., the bar following the change of signature to B major for the second time.

As Chopin has noted this passage, there is scarcely sufficient time to get in all the notes of the scale, even when, in justice to the grandeur of the passage, the player executes· it *allargando.* We would advise some such subdivision as the following :—

Observe that the player should allow himself a very short breathing space afrer the *ffz* chord, and begin the shake *mezzo forte.*

113. NOCTURNE, Op. 9, No. 2, the cadenza near the end.

Alterations in the time-value of the notes of a cadenza for which a *rallentando* is indicated are not to be taken literally. They are intended merely to suggest the approximate rhythmical value of the notes at that particular stage of the cadenza. Thus, the notation of the last four notes of the cadenza as quavers, in distinction to the preceding semiquavers*—

—indicates merely that the notes in question are to be played slowly. How slowly, depends on the graduation of the *rallentando* during the preceding notes.

---

* Certain editions note the cadenza in demisemiquavers and semiquavers; this does not effect the argument.

This cadenza should begin slowly and quicken gradually towards the centre (*forte*), whereafter it slackens speed more and more towards the end, and emerges calmly into the penultimate bar.

114. NOCTURNE, Op. 9, No. 3, the concluding cadenza.

The time-value of the notes here suffers no change through the notation in small type; play on, therefore, as though the whole passage were noted in the normal way. Make a slight *accelerando* and *crescendo* during the first half; dwell slightly on the topmost notes, then proceed pretty rapidly, gradually slackening speed towards the end. Beware, however, of dragging the last six notes; the *tempo* of the *Adagio* must not be anticipated.

Subdivide the chord in the left hand as follows:—

From this point onwards the cadenza must be played "in one breath", *i.e.*, with smooth, steady carriage of the right hand.

115. NOCTURNE, Op. 15, No. 2.

In his book "Chopin's Greater Pianoforte Works", Kleczynski gives the following good rendering of the cadenza in bar 11—

The subdivision: 6, 8, 8, 8 is, however, equally admissible, provided that the cadenza be played "in one breath" and without the slightest accentuation. The notes must flow so naturally from the player's fingers that the listener never suspects him of subdividing them consciously at all.

The corresponding cadenza in the second part should be subdivided: 9, 9, 10, 12.

116. NOCTURNE, Op. 27, No. 1, the cadenza before the *tempo primo.*

Maintain the triple time:—

117. NOCTURNE, Op. 32, No. 1, the cadenza preceding the final recitative.

Play not too rapidly, very evenly, and without any accentuation· The delivery of the recitative is largely a matter of taste. The following version is merely a suggestion:

The recitative will speak for itself if Chopin's marks of expression are faithfully observed. For the sake of rhythmical uniformity, the value of the crotchet in the last two bars (*Adagio*) should be one and a half times that of the crotchet in the bar of $\frac{3}{2}$ time. The first bar of the *Adagio* will then consume exactly the same time as the bar of $\frac{3}{2}$ time.

118. NOCTURNE, Op. 48, No. 2, the penultimate bar.

Do not begin the scale too late, otherwise the bar will lose its rhythmical balance.   The following subdivision is, we think, of good effect :—

119. NOCTURNE, Op. 62, No. 1.

First cadenza. (Bar 26.)

This bar is marked *rallentando*.   As all the notes of the cadenza are played at a uniform speed (*presto*), it follows that the quavers in the left hand must successively have more and more notes allotted to them as the *rallentando* progresses.   The subdivision given in most editions—8, 8, 13, 12—is obviously not a graduated *rallentando* at all, and could be made to sound like one only by capricious slackenings or quickenings of the notes played by the right hand.   Subdivide therefore somewhat as follows: 6+8+12+15.

The melody notes in the tenor :

are *marcato* and *non legato*.*

---

* Melodies in the tenor register of the pianoforte, when accompanied by figuration in the right hand, very often acquire a more penetrating, emotional character when played *non legato*.   This is true no matter whether the pedal be taken or not.

cf. the tenor melody in the middle section of the ETUDE, Op. 25, No. 5.

Poco più lento, bar 3.

Subdivide: 6+8+8+8, but play the last group *rubato*:

120. NOCTURNE, Op. 62, No 2, bars 30—31.

The eighth bar after *a tempo*:

121. BALLADE in F minor, Op. 52, the cadenza that concludes the exposition.

Very delicately and with an arch expression. The phrasing suggested above should be only slightly indicated.

122. IMPROMPTU, Op. 36, the cadenzas in the first section.

No. 1: 5+5+5+5. (Not on any account 6+4+5+5, as given in some editions.)

No. 2: *v.* Example 110.

123. FANTASIA in F minor, Op. 49, the recitative near the end.

The direction "*cres.*" is not superfluous; it refers to the entire passage and is cancelled eventually by the direction "*smorzando*". The additional ━━ and ━━ marks are a case of "wheels within wheels".

124. ETUDE, Op. 25, No. 5, the concluding bar.

The first few notes *ritenuto*, then *accelerando* towards the centre, and thence *allargando* towards the end. The last few notes must be delivered with the utmost force. Observe how well this consorts with the expression marks ━━ ━━━.

125. ETUDE, Op. 25, No. 7, the cadenzas in the left hand (small notes).

No. 1. As in the first example from the NOCTURNE, Op. 62, No. 1, the grouping of the notes must be proportionate to the decrease in speed. The slower the *tempo*, the more notes must we allot to each beat. Subdivide therefore: 8+8+9+9+12+12, and slacken the *tempo* additionally during the last group of 12 notes, in the interests both of clearness and of the *rallentando*.

No. 2: 8+9+8+8. There is no *rallentando* here.

126. PRELUDE, Op. 28, No. 24, the final cadenza.

This is the Niagara of cadenzas. Dwell a little on the opening notes, then rush downwards with torrential speed.

Play the first eight notes with the right hand, and the remainder in groups of four with the left and right hand alternately. The lowest note falls to the left hand.

127. PRELUDE, Op. 45.

The long cadenza should be played *leggierissimo* and as rapidly as is consistent with clearness. It is very difficult and requires careful memorizing.

128 Allegro de Concert, Op. 46.

First cadenza

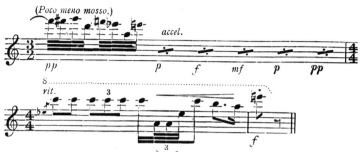

Two bars later:

[Compare this with Chopin's version of the parallel passage in bars 180—182, where we are evidently meant to play:—

Stretto = dwell on the first few notes, then pass to demisemiquavers.

Eleven bars later:—

Two bars farther on:

A considerable amount of rhythmical " give-and-take " is necessary for the performance of this entire passage.

129. CONCERTO, Op. 11, first movement.

The execution of this is approximately :

SECOND MOVEMENT.

In the fairy passage leading to the last repetition of the principal theme :

the grace notes have the value of demisemiquavers and are anticipated.

130. CONCERTO, Op. 21, the 24th bar after the "*a tempo, con anima*", where we are intended to play as follows:

Second movement, near the end of the recitative middle section:

CHAPTER XXII.

THE "INCORPORATED CADENZA."

IF, in the previous chapter, we encountered cadenzas which, so far as their execution is concerned, might equally well have been noted and barred regularly, it is on the other hand possible to cite examples of the converse kind,—passages which, although incorporated in the text and noted in the ordinary way, are really cadenzas in disguise. These latter—they might be called " Incorporated Cadenzas "—serve in Chopin's large works either to round off a section or to bridge the gap between one theme or group of themes and the next. They usually consist of one harmony expanded, in the style of which Chopin is a master, unto an arabesque or cadenza covering a large expanse of the keyboard. Here are some examples in outline :—

131. BALLADE, Op. 47, bar 33, &c.

132. BALLADE, Op. 52, bars 72—78.

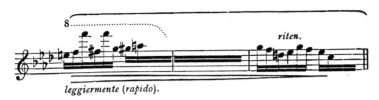

leggiermente (*rapido*).

133. FANTASIA, Op. 49, the passage leading to the *Lento sostenuto*.

In the above passages, Chopin has given explicit directions regarding the modifications of the *tempo*. Profiting by this hint, we shall play the episode leading to the second subject in the first movement of the Sonata, Op. 58, not in strict time, but with a lavish *accelerando-ritenuto* :—

134.

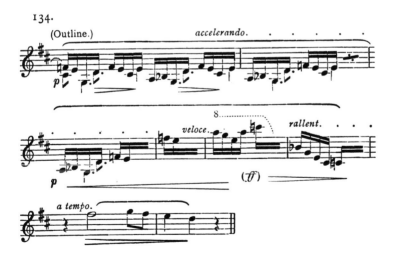

It is obvious that "incorporated cadenzas" of the above type
bear a radical resemblance to some of the cadenzas discussed
in the foregoing chapter, and must not be played in the same
way as the thematic contents of the work.   Indeed, it should be
pointed out that a pianist who aspires to become a Chopin
interpreter must learn above all to discriminate between the
essential (thematic) ingredients of a work and those which are
merely episodic or ornamental, for in no composer does a lack
of the sense of formal proportion on the performer's part make
itself more disagreeably felt.   Long-windedness and ponderosity
are an offence in the performance of any composer's works ; in
Chopin, they are a crime.   Almost all passages of the above
type, then, should be treated succinctly.   *Rubato* is essential :
the *tempo* is usually accelerated during the first half of the
passage and rectified by a compensating *rallentando* during the
latter.   Moreover, like so many of the cadenzas printed in small
type, they should be delivered "in one breath"—that is, with a
steady hand and unbroken smoothness—or they will create an
impression of toilsome clambering, woefully at variance with the
spirit of a composer whose lightness of touch never deserts him
even in his grandest, loftiest moods.

INDEX

OF

QUOTATIONS AND REFERENCES.